Copyright 2019 by Nikki Fotheringham

All rights reserved. No part of this book may be reproduced in any form without written permission from the publisher.

Published by Greenmoxie in the town of Warkworth ON, Canada

www.greenmoxie.com

Designed by Jib Limited. Photography by Gary Mulcahey

ISBN 978-0-9939954-4-6

First Edition

Food on Fire
CAMPFIRE COOKBOOK

NIKKI FOTHERINGHAM

Contents
OFF THE GRILL

Introduction..7

BREAKFAST

Bacon Breakfast Roll......................15
Skillet Blueberry Muffins..................17
French Toast Pigs in a Blanket............19
Baked Avocado................................21
Bacon and Tomato Skewers..............23
Cattail Pollen Pancakes.....................25
Fry Bread Brekkie............................27
Chorizo Hash..................................29
The Happy Bear..................................30

LUNCH

Pizza Cones....................................35
Hot Ham and
Pineapple Sandwich.........................37
Tramezzini......................................39
Toasted Sarnies...............................41
Buddha Barley Bowl.........................43
Crustless Quiche.............................45
Rainbow Pinwheels..........................47
Corn Flake Chicken Fingers...............49
Chickpea Burgers............................51
Sherry Sausage Dogs......................53
Punked by Nature..................................55

DINNER

Trout and Crunchy Potato Pie..................63
Campfire Pizza.................................65
Stew and Dumplings........................67
Bacon-wrapped Beef Medallions.............69
Peanut Butter Pasta.........................71
Beer-battered Fish
and Tornado Potatoes.......................73
Yummy Salmon Fishcakes....................75
Schnitzel Fitz...................................77
Steak and Onion Braai Pie.................79
Spit Roasted Rabbit 81

DESSERT

Blueberry Grunt	85
Campfire Cheesecake	87
Campfire Apple Crumble	89
Peach Bake	91
Cherry Hand Pies	93
Balsamic Strawberry Bake	95
Lattice Pancakes	97
Apple Cinnamon Tacos	99
Campfire Cobbler	101
Shits & Giggles	**102**
The Case of the Underwear-Clad Exchange student	**104**

ON THE SIDE

Beer Cheese Dip	109
Potato Smash	111
Fiddleheads	113
Bacon-wrapped Onion Rings	115
Bannock	117
Campfire Skillet Cornbread	119
South African Cornbread	121
Baking Soda Bread	123
Braided Campfire Bread	125
Smoky Campfire Beans	127
Burnt Tomatoes	129
More Hot Tips	**130**
How to Fillet a Fish	**131**
How to Clean a Fish	**131**

Hail the nature lover; those denizens of the deep woods who hike, bike, run, swim, row and climb so they can carpe the hell out of every diem. To the late-night lake swimmers and the daisy chain weavers. To the rain dancers, the star gazers and the mosquito slappers. To the marshmallow roasters and pokers of campfires. To all who brave the weather, the bugs and the bears to commune with nature and drink el fresco…
I salute you!

Every brave soul that takes the path less traveled should be rewarded. And with this book, I hope to do just that. This is a collection of my very best recipes curated into an essential camping cookbook—the only one you'll ever need—that will make you so damn popular, you'll never camp alone again.

One essential ingredient in a successful campfire meal is a good campfire story. I've peppered this book with stories based on true events. Some of these happened to me and some to campers I've shared a fire with. Needless to say, names have been changed to protect the innocent and downright stupid.

So, let's gather up the firewood and make some memorable meals together.

Greenmoxie.com

Is my fire ready?

Cooking times are subjective enough in a kitchen, but out in the woods, it's a little fast and loose. Here's a comprehensive guide to building a cooking fire and keeping the temperature just right.

Unless you're searing a steak on a very hot fire, you're going to need two fires to regulate temperature. Make a large fire on one side of your fire pit, and then cook on the other side. That will allow you to move coals over to the cooking area from your fire. Regulating the temperature will ensure your food comes out perfectly.

I like to make a round fire pit for my feeder fire and then two rows of rocks that lead off from that for a cooking channel. This makes it easier to rest your grill on and less likely for it to slip off.

WHAT DO WE MEAN BY HOT, MEDIUM OR COOL FIRES?

Hold your hand 10 cm (4 inches) above the coals until it gets too hot.

2-3 seconds:
This is a HOT fire! You can cook steak on this perfectly.

3-4 seconds:
A MEDIUM to HOT fire that can work for steak and chicken.

5-7 seconds:
The coals are at MEDIUM heat. Breads, puddings and frying veggies are all done at this temperature.

9 seconds:
Put some more wood on the fire, sit back and enjoy a drink with friends.

How to Make a Campfire

It sounds easy enough right? Match, wood... no brainer. But after thirty minutes on your knees huffing and puffing only to have your paltry fire smolder out, you know the struggle. Every seasoned fire starter will swear by their particular method, but there are some basic tenants that are true for all fires.

- Never use green or wet wood. That means you never tear bark or branches off living trees. Find deadfall to use or pack in your firewood.
- Birch bark makes the best natural fire starter. It's practically invincible.
- Never use fuel on a cooking fire. You're better than that.
- If the wood is very dry, you can pack up the whole fire and then toss in a match and walk away. Don't look back; badasses never do. Actually, look back... fires are dangerous!
- If the wood is not well seasoned or it has been raining, start really small. Just a little birch bark and a few small twigs, then slowly build it up. Pack the rest of the wood close to the fire so it can dry.
- Oxygen; you need it, fires need it. Always pack your kindling with gaps so the air can get in. If your fire is struggling, blow gently on kindling.
- Fire starters can be made from candle wax and dryer lint; just put the lint in the bottom of an egg carton and pour melted wax over it. Break off each egg section and use to light your fire.
- In a pinch, crayons and corn chips (like Dorritos) work really well too.

BUILDING A SNACK FIRE

This is a good one for boiling water or cooking smores and will work nicely for heat too. It's quick and easy. Place a couple of balled up pieces of paper or some birch bark in the center, then lay the kindling around in a teepee style. If the wood is wet, start small. Leave gaps between the kindling so air can get in. Light the paper or bark and blow gently on the flames.

BUILDING A COOKING FIRE

Place the bark or paper in the center with a little kindling on it. Now build a square around the kindling in a 'log cabin' formation, alternating parallel logs which leave gaps for air to get in.

You can make a ring of stones around the main fire & then a channel with parallel rows of stones coming off one side of your stone fire circle. This is your cooking area. Use a stick to scrape your coals over to the cooking channel. This means you can continue to generate hot coals in your fire & move them over to the cooking area when you need them. This helps you to regulate the temperature and you won't get caught with a dying fire and an uncooked breakfast.

Wakey, Wakey...

GOOD MORNING SUNSHINE!

BACON BREAKFAST ROLL
(You had me at bacon!)

Serves: 4

Ingredients

- 1 pack of bacon
- 2 potatoes (diced)
- 4 eggs
- 4 tbsp oil
- 1 onion (sliced)
- 1 cup cheese (sliced or shredded)

HOT TIPS:

If you are backwoods camping, freeze the bacon and wrap it in newspaper to keep it fresh for longer. You can leave out the eggs and add other vegetables like peppers, lentils and tomatoes to bulk it out.

You can add any additional filling here like mushrooms, chorizo, bell peppers, chillies and beans. Omit an egg for every additional filling ingredient.

Method

1. Roll out foil on a flat surface. Divide the pack of bacon in two (usually about five pieces in each pile). Lay half the pieces vertically on your foil so that they are touching each other. Now take one of the pieces of bacon from your second pile and weave it over and under the strips you laid down. Continue with the rest of the bacon so you make a bacon lattice that is relatively square.

2. Rinse the diced potatoes in cold water to prevent them from sticking to your pan. Place your oil in a skillet and heat over a medium fire. Add the potatoes and fry for 3 minutes or until they just start to change color.

3. Add your onions and fry until they start to soften (about 5 minutes). Test your potatoes to make sure they are cooked through.

4. Add the egg and scramble the mixture together. Spoon the egg mixture onto the middle of your bacon lattice. Leave a little space on each end. Now use the foil to fold the ends of the lattice over the top of your egg mixture. Tuck the ends of the bacon in all the way around.

5. Wrap the foil over the top and turn up the sides so that the breakfast roll is sealed in foil. Cook on a medium fire for 10 minutes on each side. Like your bacon crispy? Of course you do! Open the foil and gently roll the breakfast roll onto the grill and brown on both sides. Slice and serve immediately.

SKILLET BLUEBERRY MUFFINS (V)

Serves 6

This is amazing for brekkie, but you can enjoy this sweet dish any time. Tea time, elevensies, dessert—it's always the perfect time for muffins!

Ingredients

- 1 ½ cups flour
- ¾ cup sugar
- ½ tsp salt
- 2 tsp baking powder
- 1 cup oil
- ½ cup milk
- 1 ½ tsp vanilla
- 1 cup blueberries

Method

Mix dry ingredients in a large bowl or camping pot. Add milk, oil and vanilla essence and mix well. Add blueberries and mix until evenly distributed. The mixture will be quite thick. Pour into the bottom of a Dutch oven or camping pot and place on a medium fire. Put the lid on and place a couple of coals on the lid for an even bake and a nice brown top. Bake for about 20 minutes or until a knife stuck into the middle comes out clean. Slice and serve.

HOT TIPS:

Backwoods campers can use evaporated milk or powdered milk instead of fresh dairy.

Mix the dry ingredients before you leave on your camping trip and place in a sealable plastic bag so they take up less space in your pack.

Use vanilla-flavored sugar if you don't want to have to pack in vanilla essence.

(V) substitute almond milk for milk for a delicious brekkie.

Breakfast

FRENCH TOAST PIGS IN A BLANKET *Serves 6*

This is a really fun way to eat toast, eggs and sausages and tastes better if you eat it with your hands… mmmm sticky fingers.

Ingredients

- 6 breakfast sausages
- 2 eggs
- maple syrup
- 6 slices of bread
- 2 tbsp oil

Method

Place the oil in your camping skillet and heat over a medium fire. Fry the sausages until brown, then remove from the pan and set aside. In a bowl or camping pot, beat the eggs. Dip a slice of bread into the eggs, then pop a sausage in the middle of the bread and fold it over around the sausage. Fry in the remaining oil over a medium fire. Fry the french toast pigs in a blanket on both sides until golden brown—about 5 minutes. Serve hot drizzled with maple syrup.

HOT TIPS:

Dip the bread in the egg, don't soak it or it will break when you fold it around the sausage.

If you aren't eating this on the first day, freeze the sausages and wrap them in newspaper before placing them in your pack so they stay fresh for longer.

BAKED AVOCADO (V)

Serves 4

Healthy, hearty and the perfect fuel for a busy day. If you aren't in the backwoods, add sour cream, cheese, salsa, hot sauce or all of the above!

Ingredients

- 2 large ripe avocados
- 4 eggs
- 2 tbsp oil
- salt and pepper

Method

Slice the avos in half and remove the pit. With a spoon, scoop out enough of the center to make space for an egg. Break an egg into each avo half and season with salt and pepper. Wrap in foil with the seam on the top so you can peek in to see how your egg is doing. Cook over a medium fire for 20 minutes or until egg is done to your preference.

HOT TIPS:

If you aren't eating this on the first day, choose green avos so they can ripen on your trip.

(V) Omit the eggs and add sliced peppers or vegan cheese to fill out the avocados.

Breakfast

BACON AND TOMATO SKEWERS

Serves 6

Easy as pie, this recipe is perfect for beginner fire foodies.

Ingredients

- 36 cherry tomatoes
- 6 slices of bacon
- 6 wooden skewers soaked in water
- salt and pepper

> **HOT TIPS:**
> Maple syrup drizzled over this will be amazing!

Method

Place a skewer through the end of a slice of bacon, then pierce a cherry tomato on top of that. Wrap bacon around the tomato and then pierce it on the skewer. Alternate between layers of bacon and cherry tomatoes until the skewer is full. Barbecue over a hot fire, turning regularly until the bacon is brown—about 5 minutes. Season with salt and pepper.

CATTAIL POLLEN PANCAKES (V)

Serves 4

Cattail pollen can be collected in the spring when the cattail flower forms above the cattail seed. It looks like two cattails are growing on the same stalk, but the top one is yellow. Simply put a bag over the cattail and shake to collect the pollen. You can keep it in a dry, sealed container until you need it. Cattail pollen can be a 1:1 substitute for flour and has many nutritious benefits including manganese, vitamin K, magnesium, dietary fiber, iron, vitamin B6 and sodium.

Ingredients

- 1 ¾ cups flour
- ¼ cup cattail pollen
- 1 tsp baking powder
- 1 tsp salt
- ¼ cup oil
- 2 cups water
- oil for frying
- maple syrup

Method

Mix ingredients in a bowl and then drop spoonfuls of batter into a lightly oiled skillet over a medium fire. When the pancakes start to bubble (about 4 minutes), flip them over and cook on the other side until they are golden brown—about another 2 minutes. The cattail pollen will give your pancakes a vibrant yellow color. Drizzle with maple syrup and serve hot.

HOT TIPS:

Add blueberries or cinnamon to create flavored pancakes.

FRY BREAD BREKKIE (V)

Serves 6

Fry bread is a form of bannock (Bannock recipe page 111). This simple dough can be turned into the most delicious sweet or savory meal. If you add blueberries and sugar to the dough and drown your fry bread in maple syrup, you can have a delicious sweet breakfast treat. Or add cinnamon sugar for breakfast doughnuts.

Ingredients

- 4 cups flour
- 2 tsp baking powder
- 2 tsp salt
- 3 tbsp oil
- 1 cup warm water
- 6 slices bacon (fried)
- 6 eggs
- oil for frying

> **HOT TIPS:**
>
> Fry bread can be topped with just about anything. If you are at the start of your camping trip, eggs, bacon and cheese make the perfect breakfast.
>
> (V) If you are backcountry camping, top with peanut butter and jam or cinnamon and sugar.

Method

1. Mix dry ingredients. Add oil and enough water to form a firm dough that doesn't stick to the hands. Leave to rest for 30 minutes.
2. Divide into six portions and flatten with the palm of your hand to form discs. Poke a hole in the center to allow the oil to bubble through.
3. Heat the oil in a frying pan over a medium fire. Drop the fry bread in and cook for 2 minutes or until the edges turn brown. Turn over and fry for another 2 minutes.
4. Use remaining oil to fry eggs. Top each fry bread with a slice of bacon cut in half and a fried egg.

Breakfast

CHORIZO HASH (V)

Serves 4

Chorizo is the camper's friend. This delectable cured meat is slow to spoil and a great source of protein and flavor no matter how far you are off the beaten track.

Ingredients

- 1 cup chorizo sausage (sliced)
- 1 onion (diced)
- 1 red pepper (diced)
- 2 medium potatoes (diced)
- oil for frying

Method

Gently heat oil over a medium fire. Fry potatoes until cooked through—about 10-15 minutes. Add onions and fry until translucent and then add peppers and chorizo and fry for another 5 minutes. Serve hot.

HOT TIPS:

If you don't want the potatoes to stick, boil them for a couple of minutes and then drain the water thoroughly before frying. Make sure the oil is properly heated before adding the potatoes.

The chorizo is salty and spicy, but feel free to add other spices like turmeric and garlic if you wish.

Chorizo keeps well which makes it perfect for backcountry campfires, but if you are on the first day of your camping trip, you can use sausage or bacon instead.

(V) Omit the chorizo and add cubed tofu instead.

The Happy Bear

Canadian winters are long and hard. Once the snow melts, the city is a stark place where grey buildings and leafless trees offer no respite. There's always that stubborn stretch of hard-packed ice along the curb; black with soot and studded with cigarette butts. I was staring at that ice, willing spring to come soon. Desperate times call for desperate measures, so I booked our first camping trip - eager to get the season started.

My husband and I hauled up boxes of camping equipment from their hiatus in the basement and packed what we needed. My neighbor brought over some 'special' brownies that had a distinct green sheen. "For your camping trip," he said with a wink.

We planned an easy three-hour hike into a spot that had a beautiful view of Georgian Bay. The start of the week had been unseasonably warm but, by the time we arrived at the parking lot of the national park, the weather had taken a turn for the worse.

That did not deter the army of horseflies that constituted our greeting party. From the moment we stepped from the car, they swarmed us. The horsefly is the loudest of the biting insects—a sound that cannot be ignored and is difficult to tolerate. Their bite is painful too. They are slow, particularly in cold weather, but swatting them brings no joy at the sickening, wet crunch of their juicy bodies under your fingers.

The horseflies were driving us balmy, it was freezing cold and, by the time we reached the campsite, a fine drizzle had set in. Not wanting to add being wet to our growing list of complaints, we quickly set up camp and dived into our tent. My husband's pack and our boots went into the tent's vestibule to keep dry and we used my pack as a head rest. We crawled into our sleeping bags and tried to warm up.

One game of Yahtzee turned into five, then we decided to read. I'm not sure exactly when it happened, but at some point in the afternoon we both drifted off.

Suddenly, I woke with a start. It was pitch dark. I was sitting bolt upright in the tent before I'd opened my eyes.

A grunt and scratching, the sound of claws on fabric—it was a bear! We were both scrambling to get out of sleeping bags, yelling at the top of our lungs while feeling around frantically for headlamps. So much for playing dead.

In the early spring, bears wake ravenous from their winter hibernation at a time where there isn't a lot of food around. They are hungry and dangerous.

We zipped open the tent flap, headlamps trained through the door to reveal the retreating flanks of a big black bear. We paused, kneeling at the tent door, our hearts racing. We jumped from the tent and made as much noise as we could; yelling and shouting as we jumped about on the sharp rocks without our boots on.

When the adrenaline wore off, we tried to take stock of the damage. The backpack in the vestibule had all our food in it. The top had been pulled open, but nothing seemed to be missing except the camping pot in its little bag.

We grabbed some snacks for dinner and then packed up the bags and stomped off to the treeline to hang them, talking loudly and jumping at every sound. I shone the flashlight around in a big arc while my husband fiddled with the ropes. Finally, we were able to hoist the bags up and beat a hasty retreat to the tent.

A night of fitful sleep passed and we rose at first light to the sun breaking through the clouds. We decided to see if we could find our pot to make some morning coffee. The soft mud outside the tent was dotted with bear prints, and they are easy enough to follow. Just up the trail, I picked up a granola bar wrapper. I bet the bear really liked that snack!

Next was the bag that the pot came in and then the pot itself, flung off into the woods. I went to retrieve it and noticed a ripped piece of parchment paper. I picked it up puzzled—what was this from? Then it hit me; the brownies!

I think about that bear often and wonder how he spent the day. Was he laying in a field somewhere contemplating his paws, or did he get the munchies and wish that he'd saved that granola bar?

Munchin' on your luncheon!

Whether you are taking a brief reprieve from an active day or simply rolling out of the hammock for a bite to eat, don't let it be a handful of trail mix or a can of salty soup. You're better than that! These easy recipes are delightfully delicious and will have you munchin' on your luncheon in no time at all.

PIZZA CONES

Serves 6

We're about to do unnatural things to your favorite pie, so pizza purists look away. Eating a cone filled with all your favorite pizza toppings? Can I get a hell yeah!?

Ingredients

- 6 tortillas
- pizza sauce (pasta sauce or canned tomato sauce works too!)
- 1 cup mozzarella cheese (grated)
- 1 cup sliced pepperoni (or pizza toppings of your choice)
- water

Method

Lay the tortillas out on a sheet of foil and smear with pasta sauce, leaving the edges clear. Sprinkle a thin layer of cheese over the sauce. Add toppings and then add another thin layer of cheese. Take care not to fill it too much. Dip your finger in water and run it around the edge of the tortilla – this well help your cone stick together. Roll the tortilla into a cone shape and wrap it up with foil so it keeps its shape. Bake on each side for 5 minutes. Remove foil and grill on both sides until the tortilla is crispy and the cheese has melted.

HOT HAM & PINEAPPLE SANDWICH Serves 6

Oh hello lovers of Hawaiian pizza… I see you sitting there! These will be your new favorite sandwiches of all time. Haters are gonna hate, but know that I love you, pineapple people.

Ingredients

- 6 burger buns
- 6 slices ham
- 6 pineapple rings
- 6 slices cheese
- mustard

Method

Slice the buns open and place each one on a square of foil. Spread mustard on the bottom and top of each bun. Place the ham on the bottom, then pineapple with the cheese on top. Wrap in foil and place on a grill over a medium fire. Cook for 20 minutes until the cheese is melted. Unwrap and enjoy.

> **HOT TIPS:**
>
> Add honey if you like honey mustard.
>
> Too much pineapple? Cut the rings in half.

TRAMEZZINI

Serves 4

This is the South African take on these traditional Italian sandwiches but it's oh so delicious! It's a firm favorite in my house whenever we have leftover barbecue chicken.

Ingredients

- 4 large tortilla wraps
- 1 cup cheese (grated)
- 4 tbsp mayonnaise
- 4 chicken breasts (cooked and sliced)
- 4 tbsp oil
- salt and pepper

HOT TIPS:

This works really well with leftover barbecued chicken. Plan this lunch for the day after you have chicken on the campfire.

Method

1. Mix the sliced chicken breast and mayonnaise with the salt and pepper in a bowl. Lay out two of the large wraps and divide the chicken evenly between them, making sure you have the chicken and mayonnaise mixture evenly spread over the wraps. Sprinkle ½ cup of cheese over each wrap and put the remaining wrap on the top.

2. Place 2 tbsp of oil in a pan and heat gently over a medium fire. Carefully place one wrap "sandwich" in the pan and cook gently on one side for 5 minutes or until the wrap begins to brown. Turn over and cook on the other side for 5 minutes or until brown. Slice in quarters and serve hot.

TOASTED SARNIES

Serves 2

One of my greatest disappointments as a child was learning that sandwiches contained neither sand nor witches. Still, I've made peace with the humble sarnie and it is now an almost daily companion. We spend time together, sandwiches and I, and we understand one another. Here are some of the most wonderful sarnies you will eat in your life (true story).

Ingredients

- 4 slices of bread
- 2 tbsp butter
- 2 tbsp mayonnaise
- 1 tomato (sliced)
- 1 onion (sliced)
- 2 cheese slices
- salt and pepper

Method

Smear mayonnaise on all 4 slices of bread. Lay slices of tomato and onion on two sides and season with salt and pepper. Top with cheese slices and close sandwiches. Secure with cotton thread so they won't fall apart on the grill. Butter both sides of each sandwich on the outside. Grill over a medium fire until the bread browns and cheese melts—about 3-5 minutes.

HOT TIPS:

Add avocado for a more delicious sandwich.

This also works really well with chicken and mayonnaise.

BUDDHA BARLEY BOWL (V)

Serves 4

I don't want to build up this bowl too much, but it will be the most friggin' incredible thing you put in your mouth ever… just saying.

Ingredients

- 1 ½ cups barley
- 2 beef stock cubes
- 4 cups water
- 1 small onion (chopped)
- ½ pack bacon (chopped)
- 2 tbsp oil
- salt and pepper
- avocado
- red pepper

Method

Place the barley, beef stock cubes and water in a pot and cook over a medium fire until soft, about 30 minutes. Keep an eye on the barley, it soaks up water and you don't want it to dry out. Fry the onions and bacon in the oil until the bacon is crispy. Mix the onion, bacon and barley and top with sliced red pepper and avocado. Season with salt and pepper.

HOT TIPS:

If you are going on a long trip, substitute chorizo for the bacon and take an unripe avocado so it will last longer.

If you are going on a shorter trip or have access to a cooler or fridge, you can really experiment with this dish. Add extra veggies like grated beets, sliced zucchini and baby arugula.

For proteins you can use leftover barbecued chicken or steak or use salmon instead.

If you have space in your pack add a dressing which you can mix before you go. Mix 2 tsp of brown sugar, 2 tbsp of balsamic vinegar and 2 tbsp of olive oil.

Added garnishes can include toasted sunflower or sesame seeds.

(V) Use vegetable stock for a vegan option. Tofu makes a delicious substitute for the bacon.

CRUSTLESS QUICHE

Serves 6

Making pastry on a camping trip? I didn't think so. We can still enjoy a tasty quiche though.

Ingredients

- 8 eggs
- 1 cup cheese (optional)
- 2 tbsp oil
- 1 cup veggies (good options include mushrooms, onions, peppers, spinach, asparagus, zucchini or a combination of these)
- 1 cup meat (ham, chorizo, sliced sausages, leftover barbecued chicken or smoked salmon are all good options here)
- salt and pepper

HOT TIPS:

If you want it to bake well on the top, place a couple of coals on the lid when baking.

If you aren't eating this on the first day, you can omit the cheese and add a couple of tablespoons of parmesan cheese instead for flavor.

Method

Grease your camping skillet with the oil. In a bowl, beat the eggs with the salt and pepper until they are bubbly (about 1 minute). Add the veggies and meat and pour into the skillet. Bake with lid on for 20 minutes or until the center is firm when you shake the skillet.

RAINBOW PINWHEELS (V)

Serves 4

This is the perfect recipe for a couple of days in when you really start missing fresh food. These veggies keep well if you leave your backpack in the shade.

Ingredients

- 4 tortilla wraps
- 2 carrots (julienned)
- 1 red pepper
  (cut into thin strips)
- ½ red onion (thinly sliced)
- ½ cup mayonnaise
- salt and pepper to taste

Method

Spread the mayo on the wraps, then lay the veggies in alternating rows from one end to the other. Roll up and cut in slices.

HOT TIPS:

I like to use the green spinach wraps here for color but go with your gut!

Add leftover barbecued meat cut in thin strips for added protein.

Add spinach leaves or coriander if you are able to keep them fresh.

Add grated cheese for even more flavor.

Lunch

CORN FLAKE CHICKEN FINGERS

Serves 4

I love using food in ways that it was definitely not intended to be used and this corn flake chicken finger recipe is both simple and delicious. Don't have corn flakes? A bag of salt and vinegar chips will work perfectly too.

Ingredients

- 4 cups plain corn flakes
- ½ cup flour
- 1 tsp salt
- ½ tsp black pepper
- 4 boneless chicken breasts (cut into strips)
- olive oil

Method

Crush the corn flakes and mix with the flour, salt and black pepper. Place chicken strips in a bowl and drizzle with oil. Use your fingers to mix the chicken strips until they are well coated with oil. Cover the bottom of a skillet with oil and place on a medium fire. Fry the chicken strip for 6 to 8 minutes, turning often. When they are a golden brown, remove from pan and drain.

HOT TIPS:

Use the chicken strips to make chicken wraps with fresh veggies and mayonnaise.

Serve chicken strips with a salad and sweet chili dipping sauce.

CHICKPEA BURGERS (V)

Serves 6

Get your protein fix! This recipe is great for when you've been in the woods for a while and your meat supplies and fresh veggies are a distant memory.

Ingredients

- 1 can chickpeas (garbanzo beans)
- ½ onion (minced)
- ½ tsp garlic powder
- ¼ cup flour
- 6 buns
- salt and pepper to taste
- olive oil

HOT TIPS:

Add sliced tomato and lettuce to bulk this burger out.

Condiments like mayonnaise, mustard and hot sauce will also add to your burger yum.

Method

Drain the chickpeas and rinse. Add the onion, garlic powder, flour and seasoning and mash the chickpeas with a fork. Coat the inside of a skillet with oil and heat gently over a medium fire. Form the chickpea mixture into patties and fry on both sides until golden brown—about 3 to 4 minutes a side.

SHERRY SAUSAGE DOGS

Serves 4

Step aside humble hot dog, you can't compete with this. Grandma may miss that sherry, but you'll get hooked on these boozy dogs!

Ingredients

- 1 cup sherry
- 6 bangers
- 1 onion (sliced)
- 6 hot dog buns
- salt and pepper to taste
- olive oil

Method

Marinade the sausages in the sherry overnight. Place a little oil in the bottom of a frying pan and heat over a medium fire. Place the sausages in the pan and leave to cook, undisturbed for two minutes. Turn the sausages and fry until they are perfectly browned on every side—about 10-15 minutes depending on the thickness of your bangers. Remove the sausages and add a little more oil. Gently fry the onions until they start to brown—about 7 minutes. Add salt and pepper and the flour. Pour in the sherry marinade and reduce the liquid until a thick gravy forms. Place a sausage in a bun, then pour some gravy over the top and serve hot. This is going to be messy, but we like it that way!

HOT TIPS:

You can use any sausages here, even breakfast ones taste great!

Punked by Nature

I've always been both skeptical of hermits and in awe of their solitary lives. When every single one of our most innate instincts is telling us not to go into the woods alone, it is the hermit who shuns the safety of the herd to go solo.

My camping expeditions always involve groups of campers, I've never gone camping on my own. You see, I've a healthy fear of, and respect for, all things brown and furry. That includes bears, moose and cougars and would even stretch to squirrels if it was dark and one accidentally touched my leg.

But when I bought a beautiful 30-acre lot of wild Canadian woodland, I thought it was about time I embraced my inner hermit. Looking back now, it seems downright dumb to impose these ridiculous standards on ownership. It's the kind of bro-dog bravado that your friends used to get you to do stupid stuff when you were younger. And I should have known better.

I packed a couple of day's worth of food and my camera so I could take pictures of potential spots for the cabin I planned to build in the fall.

I said goodbye to my neighbor, Hal, who kindly dropped me off, and watched the car bump over the dirt road until it rounded the bend and was lost from view. There was a short driveway which marked the entrance of the property. No one had ever lived here, so there were no convenient hiking trails cut into the undergrowth. The first obstacle was a patch of cedars that grew so close together that I could hardly squeeze between the trunks. My backpack kept getting stuck and, by the time I emerged into the hardwood forest, I was scratched, hot and irritated.

Under the hardwoods, the going was much easier. There wasn't much undergrowth and I only had to contend with deadfall. I was just beginning to feel happy and smug when I felt the first sharp pinprick of pain as a horsefly found the bare back of my neck. Then another on my arm, and another and another until I had shrugged the pack off my back and was doing a mad dance to try to keep the black flies, horseflies and mosquitoes off me.

I opened my pack and dug around for the bug spray. Then a long-sleeved shirt and a hat so that by the end of it, the only exposed skin was on my face. The sunshine I had been so happy about this morning now seemed stiflingly hot.

Once I had gotten myself sorted out, the day improved 100 percent. The hardwood section of the forest was shady and beautiful, with enormous old-growth trees that must have been hundreds of years old. I found two streams that zig-zagged through the woods and a great place to camp and set up my tent. I put my pack in the tent, had some lunch and pulled out my camera.

I spent the rest of the day taking pictures, splashing in the stream and generally enjoying the hell out of it all. I was having so much fun that I completely lost track of time, it was only when the light began to fade that I decided to head back to the tent, gathering firewood as I went. Once or twice during the day I had worried that a bear may be attracted to the smell of food in my pack and I thought I should have taken the time to hang my food and set up my camp properly.

I was relieved when I got back to the tent and a cursory glance told me that the pack was still in there. I collected some birch bark and packed a fire. It was only when I went to get matches from my pack that I saw the tent moving a little. I froze.

I walked around the back of the tent to the rear door and approached with extreme caution. When I was close enough, I reached forward and opened the zipper on the door just a little and peeked in. There, sitting on the top of my pack, was a giant skunk.

I remember my brother getting sprayed when we were kids. While we all know that a skunk's spray stinks, it's not until you get up close and personal that you realize just how effective a defense mechanism it is. I could hear my brother from two blocks away. He was screaming and running home at a full sprint. As I ran to see what all the fuss was about, I was hit with a wall of smell so strong and powerful that it took my breath away and had me heaving on the front lawn, eyes streaming, bent double and trying desperately to get away from him.

> "SITTING THERE CONTEMPLATING MY LIFE WHILE THE SUN DIPPED LOWER IN THE HORIZON WAS NOT MY FINEST HOUR I HATCHED A PLAN, A HALF-BAKED ONE, BUT A PLAN NEVERTHELESS."

Horrified, he ran into the house to get help. A fatal mistake, because the house could not shake the smell of skunk for weeks. No amount of tomato juice or peroxide helped. My mother would walk around, sniffing the air suspiciously and demanding to know where the smell was coming from as though we had somehow hidden it from her.

I recoiled immediately from the tent as this childhood scene flashed through my mind. How had it gotten in? I got down on my hands and knees and peeked in under the tent's vestibule to see that I hadn't quite closed the tent zipper all the way and now it was in there, enjoying my eggs.

I didn't have a lot of options. If I scared it, it would spray my tent, and my sleeping bag and everything I owned which would make for a very unpleasant night. I decided that I really didn't need eggs after all, so I would just leave the skunk to finish its meal, then it could be on its way.

I backed off from the tent and went to sit by the fire. Oh right... I didn't have a fire because the matches were in the tent. With the skunk.

Sitting there contemplating my life while the sun dipped lower in the horizon was not my finest hour. I hatched a plan, a half-baked one, but a plan nevertheless.

I found a long, thin stick—the kind that would be perfect to roast marshmallows on—and slowly stalked the tent. Eventually I was within striking distance. I slowly slipped the tip of the stick through the zipper and started to open the zipper of the vestibule.

Mad thrashing around in the tent! I stopped immediately and waited until the ruckus died down. Then I started again, this time moving the zipper painfully slowly so that it didn't spook the skunk. A full twenty minutes went by before I had the vestibule completely open. Using the stick in the zipper, I carefully drew the loose end away from the door and laid it over the back of the tent. Now for the tent door.

I took a deep breath and tried to feed the tip of the stick through the zipper, but I accidentally touched the side of the tent, only to anger the beast within. I could see it now, through the mesh. It ran madly in a circle and, when it raised its tail. I froze... would it spray?

I held my breath and waited, but after a minute or two it backed off from the door and went back to rooting in my pack. I tried again. This time I got it. Now all I had to do was the slowest and quietest door opening in camping history.

I started slowly and got the door about halfway open when a light evening breeze moved the fabric and it got caught in the zipper.

Seriously? Are you friggin' kidding me?!

Huge sighs. Huge gargantuan sighs, but they would make no difference. OK, on to plan C. The door would just have to work the way it was.

I used my exceptional ninja stealth to sneak around the back of the tent. Using my trusty stick, I gave the tent a gentle tap on the back, hoping it would scare the skunk which would escape through the half-open door. The skunk rounded on me, baring its teeth and charged at the stick. I had no idea that they were so fierce. I'll admit that I dropped the stick and ran!

I spent a few moments in the woods before I sheepishly came back to pick up my stick and try again. I was still in front of the tent, but this time, the skunk was waiting for me. As I bent down to get the stick, it let me have it with both barrels. Twin streams of yellow stink shot out of its butt, sailed through the tent mesh and hit me dead in the face. My eyes just happened to be closed, but my mouth was not. I got skunk spray right in the mouth! In the MOUTH!

The smell took my breath away. I wiped my tongue on my sleeve and ran towards the stream, tripping over undergrowth and screaming as I went. I fell to my knees and shoved my face in, letting the ice-cold water wash over me. I dug my hands into the river sand and bought up handfuls, rubbing it over my face in an attempt to scour off the stink, but it didn't help. I washed my face for ten whole minutes until the nausea subsided. The smell was worse than anything I had ever experienced. My eyes and nose were burning, and the smell was so bad it was physically painful.

I'd had enough. I marched back to the campsite and over to the tent. The skunk was gone, of course. I packed up my tent and shoved my stinking gear into my pack. I took out my flashlight and I started off through the woods, stopping occasionally to retch into the undergrowth, never getting used to that awful smell. I made it back to the road in record time.

Marching back up the hill, I walked with one eye on my phone, waiting for the two bars I needed to make a call. When I finally got there, I called my neighbor. "Hal, you need to come get me and Hal, bring the pickup." When he asked why, I just said 'skunk" and he could tell exactly what had happened.

Hal picked me up fifteen minutes later, the windows of his pickup firmly closed as he waved to me from inside. I climbed into the back, sulking all the way home and trailing skunk stink as we went.

When I got home, I found my front door open and my bath drawn with a mixture of peroxide and dishwashing liquid, courtesy of Hal's wife, Sue. I bathed, then soaked my gear. Four times.

On hot summer's days when it gets humid and the wind blows just right, and you get that faint whiff of skunk, you can find me retching in a flower bed somewhere re-evaluating my bushcraft skills.

Campfire Dinner... Go with your Gut!

At the end of a long day of hiking, paddling, riding or relaxing, all that fresh air is bound to make you hungry. Well, we've got you covered. Campfire cooking is supposed to taste amazing, so ditch those instant noodles and let's make a fire!

TROUT AND CRUNCHY POTATO PIE

Serves 4

There's nothing like fresh fish. This recipe works with any fish, but it's best served with fresh-caught trout on a campfire next to the lake.

Ingredients

- 4 large baking potatoes
- 4 fillets of trout
  (use any other fish if you prefer)
- 4 tbsp butter
- salt and pepper to taste

HOT TIPS:

Add fresh dill and lemon juice in the summer for a fresher tasting dish.

Method

1. Grate 2 of the potatoes and squeeze some of the water out. Melt 2 tbsp of butter in a skillet and cover with the grated potato. Season with salt and pepper. Fry your potato pancake until crispy on the bottom. Turn it out onto a plate.

2. Repeat with the other two potatoes, laying the grated spuds over the melted butter to form a pancake. Season with salt and pepper.

3. Lay the fish fillets out on top of the potatoes and add the first pancake on top to make a sandwich. Cook (covered) for 15-20 minutes until the fish is done. Cut in segments like a pie.

Dinner

CAMPFIRE PIZZA

Serves 4

It's foolproof! Making delicious pizza from scratch even when you are four days into a backcountry camp is a super power that will make you the envy of all your camping friends.

Ingredients

- 1 ½ cups self-rising flour
- ½ tsp salt
- ⅓ cup warm water
- 3 tbsp olive oil
- 1 can tomato paste
- 1 medium onion (diced)
- 1 cup cheese (grated)

Method

Mix the flour, salt, warm water and olive oil into a firm pizza dough. Oil a skillet and press the dough into the bottom of the pan. Smear tomato paste on the dough and sprinkle onion over the top. Top your pizza with cheese and place over medium hot coals. Place the lid on the skillet and bake until the crust has browned around the edges (about 30 minutes) or put these straight on the grill with the skillet over the top for a crispier crust (about 20 minutes).

HOT TIPS:

Mix the dry ingredients in a sealable plastic bag before you leave. Just add the oil when you are ready for pizza magic.

Substitute fresh slices of tomato for the tomato paste if weight is an issue.

Add bacon, ham, pepperoni, mushrooms or any other pizza topping of choice.

Chorizo and pepperoni are better for backcountry camping.

If you are backcountry camping, freeze the cheese, wrap in newspaper and bury it in your clothing so that it will last longer.

STEW AND DUMPLINGS

Serves 4

Hearty and delicious, this is the perfect antidote to a cold, rainy day at the campsite.

Ingredients for the stew

- 2 tbsp oil
- 1 lb 10 oz beef (cubed)
- 2 cloves of garlic (crushed)
- 1 large red onion (diced)
- 2 large carrots (sliced)
- 2 cups beef stock
- 2 bay leaves
- 1 tsp dried thyme
- 1 tbsp balsamic vinegar
- salt and pepper to taste

Ingredients for the dumplings

- 1 cup flour
- 1 tsp baking powder
- 4 tbsp shortening
- Pinch of salt
- water (about ¼ cup)

HOT TIPS:

If you are going on a long trek and aren't making this dish at the beginning, freeze the beef to help it keep longer.

If weight is an issue, use beef stock cubes which you can add to boiling water.

Method

1. Place oil in a camping pot on a medium fire. Add beef and cook for 10 minutes or until brown on all sides. Add garlic, onion, carrots and stock. Cook for 2 minutes then add herbs, balsamic, salt and pepper.

2. Cover with a lid and cook for 1 hour or until meat is tender.

3. In a bowl mix the flour, salt and baking powder. Rub in the shortening until the mixture resembles breadcrumbs. Slowly add water until you have a dough that is stiff, but sticky. Drop spoonfuls of the dough into the stew and close the lid. Cook for 20 minutes until the dumplings are nicely risen.

BACON-WRAPPED BEEF MEDALLIONS   Serves 6

Everything is better wrapped in bacon… yes, even you.

Ingredients

- 6 (6 oz) 2-inch top sirloin fillets
- 6 slices bacon
- 4 tbsp butter
- ¼ tsp garlic salt
- salt
- toothpicks soaked in water

Method

1. Wrap each piece of beef with a slice of bacon and secure with a toothpick. Coat with butter and season with salt and garlic salt. Over a hot fire, sear one side of the steak on the grill for 3 minutes. Rotate ¼ turn and sear for another 3 minutes. Repeat on the other side. This will give you a medium rare steak (an internal temperature of 135°F), 5-7 minutes for medium (140°F) or 8-10 minutes for medium-well (150°F).

2. Leave to rest for 5 minutes before serving and remove toothpick.

HOT TIPS:

If you don't want to use butter, use oil instead.

For longer trips, freeze meats and wrap in newspaper to keep fresh for longer.

Dinner

PEANUT BUTTER PASTA (V)

Serves 4

Peanuts, pasta... perfection! This recipe has hints of pad thai, top notes of umami and a nutty after taste.

Ingredients

- 14 oz dried pasta (I like fettuccine for this!)
- 3 tbsp peanut butter
- 4 tbsp honey
- 4 tbsp soy sauce
- 3 tbsp balsamic vinegar
- 1 garlic clove (minced)
- ½ tsp grated fresh ginger root (grated)
- 3 sliced green onions (optional)

Method

I mix the peanut butter, honey, soy, vinegar, garlic and ginger in a sealable container before I leave for my trip. When you're ready to eat, boil the pasta in salty water until done. Drain the pasta and pour the sauce over the hot noodles. Garnish with green onions.

HOT TIPS:

You can bulk out this meal by adding fried onions, red peppers, green peppers, mushrooms or broccoli.

Add chopped peanuts on the top for a nice texture and some added protein.

(V) Omit the honey and buy egg-free pasta for a vegan option.

BEER-BATTERED FISH AND TORNADO POTATOES

Serves 6

A camping take on the classic fish and chips. These tornado potatoes are so damn good!

Ingredients for the fish

- 6 (4 oz) fish fillets (cod, trout and bass are my favorites)
- ½ cup flour
- 1 egg (beaten)
- ½ bottle beer
- oil for frying
- salt and pepper to taste

Method for the fish

Pour enough oil into your camping pot to cover the bottom with an inch of oil. Heat over a medium fire. Rinse fish fillets and pat dry. Mix flour with salt and pepper. Add egg and enough beer to form a thin batter. Dip the fillets in the batter and then gently drop into the oil. Fry, turning once, until they are brown on both sides, about 5-6 minutes.

Ingredients for the potatoes

- 6 whole potatoes with skins on
- 6 wooden skewers soaked in water
- 6 tbsp oil
- salt and pepper to taste

Method for the potatoes

Boil potatoes in your camping pot for 10 minutes. Remove from the water and leave until cool enough to handle. Pierce each potato with a wooden skewer. Using a sharp knife, make a small incision at the top and then rotate the potato so you continue to make a spiral cut all the way from the top to the bottom. Fan out the pieces, coat with oil and season with salt and pepper. Place potatoes on the grill over a medium fire and roast until golden brown, about 25-30 minutes.

HOT TIPS:

Fresh fish works best for this recipe, so take your fishing pole with you on your camping trip.

YUMMY SALMON FISH CAKES

Serves 4

Pirates dig these, mermaids want to be these and any scurvy dog that has sailed the seven seas would give up a peg leg just to try these.

Ingredients

- 1 lb boneless salmon fillet
- 4 large potatoes
- 1 onion (finely chopped)
- 1 egg
- panko bread crumbs
- salt and pepper
- oil
- avocado (optional)

Method

Peel, cut and boil the potatoes until they are done (about 15 minutes). Mash them with the fish and add the onion, eggs and seasoning. Mix well, then form into patties. Fill a camping plate with panko and press the fish cakes into the crumbs until they are coated. Fry over a medium fire until golden brown (about 6-8 minutes). Top with slices of avocado and serve hot.

HOT TIPS:

Any fish works with this recipe. Fresh caught is even better.

Canned fish will work if you don't have fresh. Tuna works really well with this recipe.

Left over fish and baked potatoes from last night's barbecue work extra well.

Serve with wasabi and pickled ginger for a real camping sushi experience.

SCHNITZEL FITZ

Serves 4

Ah man, so good. Just so so so so so good!

Ingredients

- 4 pork cutlets
- 4 slices ham
- 2 eggs (lightly beaten)
- 1 cup breadcrumbs
- 1 cup cheese (grated)
- 1 tsp salt
- 1 tsp pepper
- 1 tsp smoked paprika
- 4 wooden toothpicks soaked in water
- 4 tbsp oil for frying

> **HOT TIPS:**
>
> You can add extra fillings to your cheese like bacon, asparagus or onions.
>
> If your pork chops are very thick, use your water bottle to hammer them out a little. This will ensure they cook before drying out and will help tenderize your chops.

Method

Mix bread crumbs, salt, pepper and smoked paprika in a bowl and set aside. Onto each pork chop, place a slice of ham and ¼ cup cheese. Roll up the chop and secure with a toothpick. Dip in the beaten egg and roll in the seasoned breadcrumbs. Gently heat oil over a medium fire. Place pork cutlets into the warm oil and cook until golden brown, about 6-10 minutes. Serve hot.

STEAK AND ONION BRAAI PIE

Serves 6

This amazing savory pie is a favorite on South African barbecues (braais), and I am happy to share it with you! It's really simple and you can add any filling you like - spinach and feta or leftover barbecued chicken and mayo all work really well.

Ingredients

- 1 lbs steak
- ½ onion (chopped)
- ½ cup white mushrooms (sliced)
- 2 sheets puff pastry
- 1 cup cheese (grated)
- salt and pepper to taste
- oil

Method

1. Grill your steak over a medium fire 3-4 minutes per side for medium rare. Remove from the grill and leave to rest for 2 minutes. Coat the grill with oil to prevent the pie from sticking. Lay one sheet of puff pastry on the grill, then layer with onion and then mushrooms. Add a little salt and pepper to the vegetables. Thinly slice the steak and layer it over the vegetables. Top with grated cheese. Lay the last sheet of puff pastry over the top and pinch the sides all the way around the pie to prevent the filling from escaping.

2. Grill over a medium fire for 20-30 minutes or until golden brown.

HOT TIPS:

You can use just about any filling in this pie. Spinach and feta for a veggie version, leftover barbecue chicken and mayonnaise or sausage and tomato all work super well.

If you can't haul puff pastry into the woods, here's an easy recipe with vegetable shortening that you can make on the spot because it doesn't have to be kept cold.

Mix 2 cups of all-purpose flour with a tsp of salt. Rub in 1 cup of vegetable shortening and enough cold water to make a dough (about 4 tbsp). The colder the water, the better!

SPIT ROASTED RABBIT

Serves 4

Rabbit is delicious and tender when cooked on a campfire. I cook rabbit on the spit because it adds flavor and makes the outside crispy, but you can cook it any way you damn well please.

Ingredients

- 1 whole rabbit skinned and gutted
- 1 cup olive oil
- juice and zest of a lemon
- 2 sprigs of sage
- 2 sprigs of rosemary
- 2 cloves of garlic (crushed)
- 2 tsp salt
- 2 tsp pepper

Method

1. Chop up the sage and 1 sprig of rosemary. Mix the rest of the ingredients in a sealable plastic bag or container and marinade the rabbit for no longer than 4 hours. While the rabbit is marinating, make a spit and soak it in water (see tips).

2. Set up the spit and scrape coals in under it. Turn the rabbit often, using the remaining rosemary sprig to baste it with marinade every time you do.

3. Cook for 20-30 minutes over a medium fire until golden brown. The internal temperature should be 155°F (68°C)

HOT TIPS:

To make a spit, cut 2 Y-shaped sticks to hold the spit and plant one on both sides of the fire pit. Cut a spit - a long, straight stick that will go through the rabbit body cavity. I like to strip this stick of bark and soak it in water so that it doesn't catch on fire. Once you pass this spit through the body, use two small pegs through the front and back legs to secure the rabbit to the spit. Lay the spit on the two Y-shaped sticks over the fire. Turn often to avoid burning.

Just Desserts

Have your cake and eat it too! S'mores are great, but there's so much more you can do to add a little sweetness to your camping experience. Here's some delicious recipes to ease that sweet tooth.

BLUEBERRY GRUNT (V)

Serves 4

A signature dish of Nova Scotia in Canada, the blueberry grunt is a firm favorite. Delicious and easy to prepare, it's bound to become a staple on camping trips.

Ingredients

- 4 cups blueberries
- 1 ¼ cup sugar
- ½ cup water
- ½ tsp cinnamon
- 2 cups flour
- 2 tsp baking powder
- ½ tsp salt
- 2 tbsp butter
- 1 cup milk

Method

1. Combine the berries, water and 1 cup of sugar and cook over a medium fire until the mixture starts to thicken - about 10 minutes. Hot jam!

2. Combine flour, baking powder and salt and cut in the butter. Add milk until just mixed. Drop spoonfuls of the dough into your jam and put the lid on. Steam for 15 minutes. Keep the lid on so your dumplings can get all hot and steamy!

HOT TIPS:

Substitute vegetable shortening or oil for butter on longer trips.

Use canned or powdered milk if you can't keep milk fresh.

(V) Use oil instead of butter for a yummy veggie option.

Dessert

CAMPFIRE CHEESECAKE

Serves 6

Yup, you better believe it! This recipe is so easy and so great I make it at home too. You don't need refrigeration, but it can be a little mushy on hot days. Don't let that stop you, it's still going to taste amazing!

Ingredients

- 1 pack graham crackers
- 3 tbsp butter (melted)
- 3 tbsp of sugar
- 2 bricks cream cheese
- 1 can condensed milk
- 1 can cherry pie filling

Method

1. Break up the graham crackers into crumbs. Add the sugar and melted butter and mix. Press into the bottom of your skillet. You can also halve the recipe and use a camping pot instead or make individual cheesecakes in camping mugs.

2. In a bowl, mix the cream cheese and condensed milk until smooth. Pour into your skillet or pot and leave to set. Pour pie filling over the top and enjoy!

HOT TIPS:

Freeze the butter and cream cheese if it's going to be a hot day.

You can use jam or fresh fruit instead of pie filling to top off your cheesecake.

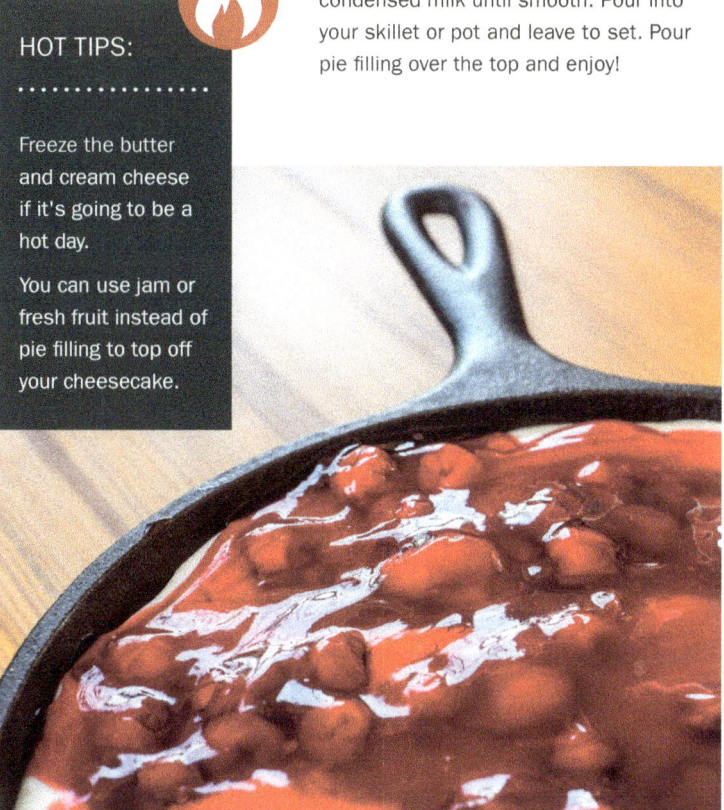

Dessert

CAMPFIRE APPLE CRUMBLE (V)

Serves 4

There's nothing finer than the humble crumble. The smoky crispness of the campfire makes this dessert a firm favorite in my neck of the woods.

Ingredients

- 4 apples (cored and cut into slices)
- ½ cup brown sugar
- ½ cup rolled oats
- ½ tsp cinnamon
- ½ tsp nutmeg
- ⅓ cup butter

Method

Place the sliced apples in a skillet or camping pot. Combine the rest of the ingredients and sprinkle over the top. Place the lid on the skillet or pot and bake over a medium fire until the apples are tender - about 20 minutes. Pop a couple of coals on the skillet lid to brown the top.

HOT TIPS:

For backpacks, mix the dry ingredients at home and place in a sealable plastic bag so that it takes up very little space.

(V) Substitute vegetable shortening for the butter if you are planning on eating this on a longer trip.

PEACH BAKE (V)

Serves 4

Simple. Perfection. Pack your peaches carefully so they don't get bruised. It will be well worth the extra effort.

Ingredients

- 6 peaches halved (peeled with pits removed)
- honey
- walnuts

Method

Cut peaches in half and remove pits. Cook on a medium campfire until done, but still firm - 4 to 5 minutes for each side. Drizzle with honey and break walnuts over the top.

HOT TIPS:

If you are car camping, whipped cream or ice cream go really well with these.

(V) Use maple syrup instead of honey for a vegan option.

CHERRY HAND PIES (V)

Serves 4

Just because you're camping doesn't mean you can't have your pie and eat it too. These sweet little treats are tasty and super easy to make. Do it!

Ingredients

- 2 cups flour
  (and a little more for dusting)
- 2 tbsp granulated sugar
  (and 2 more for dusting)
- 1 tsp baking powder
- ½ tsp salt
- 5 tbsp vegetable shortening
- 6 tbsp water
- 1 can cherry pie filling
- vegetable oil for frying

Method

1. Mix the flour, 2 tbsp of sugar, baking powder and salt together in a medium bowl. Rub in the shortening until it resembles fine breadcrumbs. Add the water, a little at a time until the dough comes together. Press it or roll it out on a clean surface dusted with flour. A water bottle makes a great rolling pin!

2. Use a cup to cut out rounds, fill with cherry pie filling and press the edges together.

3. Heat the oil in your camping pan and fry the pies on each side until golden brown, about 6-8 minutes on each side. Remove from pan and dust with remaining sugar.

HOT TIPS:

You can substitute 2 cups pitted cherries and ½ cup sugar for a fresher filling.

You can bake these in a greased Dutch oven with coals on the lid for a healthier treat.

You can use frozen pastry instead of making your own. Crescent roll pastry works well too.

If you can bring in a can of whipped cream to top these off, you'll be one happy camper!

Dessert

BALSAMIC STRAWBERRY BAKE

Serves 4

Vinegar and strawberries may not sound like something you want to put in your mouth, but then you do and it's sweet, sweet (slightly sour) heaven!

Ingredients

- 1 pint strawberries
- 2 tbsp balsamic vinegar
- 2 tbsp sugar
- 8 marshmallows
- black pepper to taste

Method

1. Hull strawberries and cut in half. Place in a bowl and add sugar and balsamic vinegar. Toss, cover and leave aside for 1 hour.
2. Roast marshmallows over a medium fire until golden brown. Dish strawberries into four servings and top with black pepper and then roasted marshmallows.

HOT TIPS:

Start this dessert before dinner so it's ready when you're done. Don't leave strawberries to marinade for more than 4 hours.

LATTICE PANCAKES

Serves 4

It matters not whether you make your own pancake batter or you use the premade mix, the presentation of these delicate, delicious desserts will make your taste buds sing.

Ingredients

- 2 cups flour
- 2 eggs
- 1 cup milk
- ¼ tsp salt
- 1 tsp sugar
- 2 tbsp butter (melted)
- maple syrup
- oil

Method

1. Place the flour, eggs, milk, salt, sugar and butter in a bowl and mix until there are no lumps. Pour the batter into a sealable plastic bag. Cut the corner off when you are ready to make the pancakes so you can slowly squeeze the batter out. Keep your camping cup handy to rest the bag in between pancakes.

2. Heat a pan over a medium fire and lightly oil. Squeeze the batter into the pan in a pattern. Cook for 45 seconds to 1 minute, or until light golden brown. Turn and cook the other side for a further 30 seconds. Stack your pancakes to keep them warm.

3. Serve on a plate and drizzle with maple syrup.

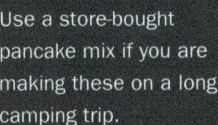

HOT TIPS:

Use a store-bought pancake mix if you are making these on a long camping trip.

If you have an empty squeezable ketchup bottle, you can use this to make interesting patterns. You can achieve the same results by pouring the batter into a plastic bag and cutting a small piece off the corner.

Of course you can add berries, or chocolate chips or bananas… or whiskey (just saying!)

APPLE CINNAMON TACOS

Serves 4

Sweet baby snakes this is a good one! The crispy taco shells combined with the sweet filling will make your toes curl.

Ingredients

- 6 small taco shells
- ½ cup cinnamon sugar
- 2 tbsp butter
- 4 apples (peeled, cored, and chopped)
- ½ cup granulated sugar
- 1 tsp ground cinnamon
- pinch salt
- oil for frying

> **HOT TIPS:**
>
> Use oil instead of the butter if you want to make this on the trail and don't have a way to keep the butter cool.
>
> If you are car camping, add some ice cream or whipped cream on top.

Method

1. Make the cinnamon shells: Cover the bottom of your camping pan with oil and heat over a medium fire until shimmering. Pop one tortilla in at a time and cook for 1 minute. Flip it over and cook for another minute. Remove from heat and coat in cinnamon sugar. Drape over a twig so you get a folded taco and leave to cool. Repeat with the other 3 tortillas.

2. Make the apple filling: In a large skillet over a medium fire, melt butter. Add apples, sugar, cinnamon and salt. Cook until the mixture is jammy—about 10 minutes. Divide the mixture in 4 and scoop into cooled taco shells.

Dessert

CAMPFIRE COBBLER

Serves 6

A firm favorite around our campfire. This recipe is just perfect for big groups or if you want cobbler for breakfast too.

Ingredients

- ½ cup old-fashioned oats
- 6 tbsp flour
- 3 tbsp packed brown sugar
- ¼ cup granulated sugar
- ¼ tsp cinnamon
- 3 tbsp butter (and a little bit more for the foil)
- 1 ½ cups blueberries

Method

Before you leave, combine the oats, sugars, flour, and cinnamon in a sealable plastic bag. When you are ready to enjoy your cobbler, add the butter to the dry ingredients and rub in until it's crumbly. In a small skillet or camping pot, layer your blueberries on the bottom and then sprinkle the oats mixture over the top. Bake over a medium fire for 20 minutes. Tent foil or a larger pot over your cobbler for a crispy, browned top.

HOT TIPS:

Substitute 3 tbsp of coconut oil for the butter and use canned fruit like peaches, cherries or apricots if you are going on a longer camping trip.

You can also use fresh fruit like apples and pineapples.

You can cook this recipe in foil. Lay out the foil and rub with butter or oil to prevent sticking. Put the fruit down first, then sprinkle the oats mixture over the top. Tent the foil up over the cobbler and bake on the grill until golden brown (about 20 minutes).

Shits & Giggles

My wife and I had been looking forward to our camping trip for weeks. On Friday afternoon, we both left work early, tossed our already packed gear into the car and headed for the hills.

For the first night, we had selected a camping spot not far from the main parking lot because we knew we would be arriving late. A short one hour hike brought us to the edge of a beautiful lake; it's white sand beach crunched underfoot and fireflies were already starting to flit through the undergrowth. It was breathtaking.

We savored the scene for a moment, then set up camp, taking care to disturb the forest as little as possible. We made a small campfire in the firepit and were just sitting down to our dinner when our new neighbours arrived.

In order to minimize the impact on the environment, it is customary for campsites to be grouped together. There were two sites side-by-side at this location that shared an outhouse and a line to hang bags out of the reach of bears and raccoons.

Our neighbours were a rabble of boys in their late teens and early twenties. They were already drunk by the time they rolled up and my wife and I looked at each other sceptically.

We waved hello but they didn't return our greeting. Instead, they threw their bags in a pile and set about making a campfire… on the beach. They pulled a collection of knives and handsaws from their packs and began hacking off tree limbs.

I stepped up and explained that they couldn't damage trees or make a fire on the beach—offering instead the compromise of deadfall and the firepit. Hell, I even offered to collect the firewood myself.

The biggest of the eight lads stepped forward. "I'm Ollie," he said, "and this…" he made a sweeping motion with his hand. "This is my kingdom. Now why don't you just go…" insert here a few choice expletives that teenagers have a habit of overusing in an unconvincing effort to establish their badassery.

I shrugged and ambled back to my campsite. "It's going to be a long night," my wife said. We discussed options as the boys fired up their sound system and proceeded to pump out dance music at full volume. It was dark now and far too late to move to the next campsite which was a good three-hour hike away. We had no option but to wait it out until the morning.

As the full horror of the night unfolded, my wife suddenly smiled wryly. God bless that woman; she has a wicked mind for retribution. Once we'd hatched our plan for revenge, listening to the boys have a party until two in the morning didn't seem so bad.

When we rose at seven, the boys were all passed out on the beach, having never actually put up their tents. We made a leisurely breakfast, then packed up most of our gear. My wife left the camping stove and medical kit out. The last thing she did was brew Ollie a really strong cup of coffee, with the addition of a laxative from the first aid box.

She waited until the hot sun started the boys stirring. Then she went over to Ollie and offered him a cup; "You look like you could use some coffee," she said. He gladly accepted it and then she set about packing the last of our things. Taking the empty mug, she wished the boys good luck and we set off up the path.

As we reached the outhouse, we each picked up a side and moved it about four feet back.

We had barely crested the first hill when Ollie's scream of utter horror scattered the birds in a five-mile radius. We smiled at each other and went skipping on down the trail.

The Case of the Underwear-Clad Exchange Student

I was probably about twenty when I met Anka at a university mixer. Anka was a Dutch exchange student and when she walked through the door with a head of blonde curls and those azure eyes, I was one smitten kitten.

We got to talking and, when she expressed an interest in seeing the Canadian outdoors, I explained that I was a camping expert of eagle scout proportions. In truth, I had spent a couple of nights camping in the backyard with my dad. The highlight of these evenings had been peeing in the garden. "Don't tell mom," Dad would say as we liberally watered her rhododendrons.

We'd make a small fire and roast marshmallows, and always intend to stay out all night. But around one in the morning, we'd inevitably creep back inside and snuggle up in bed.

Of course, the minor detail of my complete lack of camping savvy did not deter me and I set about planning our romantic weekend away at a national park. I begged and borrowed camping gear from all my friends until I had cobbled together enough to pass as a seasoned camper.

We set out on a warm spring day with the sun shining and our spirits high. We had a short two-hour hike to the campsite and we took our time. So far, so good!

When we arrived at the campsite, Anka was so taken with the beauty of the lake that she peeled off her sweaty clothing and ran down for a swim in her bathing suit.

While I really wanted to join her, I decided to take this opportunity to set up the tent as I had never done it before and wanted to look professional. Dad's tent had just had two poles, but this tent was an old canvas affair and my heart sank as a series of metal poles clattered out of the bag and onto the ground. There were no instructions, the poles all looked alike and I didn't even know what shape the tent should be.

I sprang into action, but by the time Anka had finished her swim, I hadn't make any progress.

"Do you need help?" she asked sweetly, but I shook my head. I put on a philosophical look and gazed thoughtfully off into the woods while my mind raced, trying to find a way to save this dismal situation.

"You know," I said. "The stars are particularly pretty this time of year, so let's camp in true Canadian style, out in the open around the fire. Unless of course, you're not up for it…" Genius! I gave myself a little mental pat on the back.

"Of course," She smiled. "That sounds very romantic."

That night we cooked over the open fire, roasted the prerequisite marshmallows and curled up in our sleeping bags on opposite sides of the campfire. It was quite cold, but the stars were indeed beautiful and Anka was suitably impressed.

With all that fresh air, it wasn't long until I dozed off. I was in a deep sleep when I was suddenly awoken by a terrible buzzing. An enormous swarm of mosquitos had found the only piece of exposed skin (my face) and were launching an attack of epic proportions.

I panicked and screamed, and rolled over, slapping my face to get rid of them. As I rolled, the edge of my sleeping bag fell in the fire and the nylon lit up like a Christmas tree.

Anka was already up and on it, and she simply rolled me and my sleeping bag down the bank and into the lake.

There was some choice language and a lot of splashing about, but finally I emerged from the lake; wet and covered in lake weeds, dragging my sorry little sleeping bag behind me.

Anka was waiting by the campfire with a towel. She laughed and held it out to me and then built up the campfire while I did what I could to dry off. She laid my sleeping bag out to dry, then got a headlamp from her pack.

While I warmed up around the fire, Anka made short work of setting up the tent. I was wishing the earth would swallow me up by the time she returned to the campfire.

"Look Anka," I started. "I'm sorry, but I don't really know anything about camping. I just wanted to impress you. I'll just sit out here until the morning, then I'll give you a ride back to the city. I'll understand if you don't want to see me again."

Anka laughed and shook her head. "Don't be silly," she said. "The weekend has just begun and it doesn't matter that you know nothing about camping—I'll be happy to show you. And you don't have to sit out here all night. The tent is warm and cozy and, if you like, you can share my sleeping bag."

Needless to say, that was the best camping trip of my life.

On the Side...

While your main dish may be the star of the show, those sides sure do make a meal. Campfire dinners don't traditionally have side dishes, but there's no real reason for that. Here are some simple, delicious sides that will take your campfire cooking to the next level.

BEER CHEESE DIP

Serves 8

Beer Cheese Dip. If this isn't the best sentence ever written, I don't know what is! All of your favorite things combine to make a party in your mouth.

Ingredients

- 3 cups cheddar cheese (shredded)
- 8 oz of softened cream cheese
- 2 cloves of minced garlic
- 1 cup lager beer
- 1 tbsp fresh chives (or green onion)
- ¼ tsp cayenne pepper
- salt

Method

Mix the cheddar and cream cheese with garlic, chives and beer in the skillet. Season with the salt and cayenne pepper. Cover the skillet with foil. Place the skillet over hot coals and wait until the mix melts. Occasionally stir using a wooden cooking spoon. Once the cheese had melted, serve with bread, pretzels or crackers.

POTATO SMASH (V)

Serves 4

This is a great way to cook potatoes on a campfire that leaves them crispy and so delicious you may just give up french fries for these…

Ingredients

- 8 small russet potatoes
- 2 tbsp oil
- 4 tsp butter
- 8 tsp parmesan cheese
- salt and pepper to taste

Method

Place potatoes in a pot of cold water on the fire and gently boil until soft, but still firm. Drain. Before the potatoes cool, place them on a hard surface with a dish towel over the top and press down until they smash open. Place oil in a pan and heat over a medium fire. Add the potatoes and top each one with ½ tsp butter, 1 tsp parmesan cheese and salt and pepper to taste. Fry gently until crisp and serve hot. To get the top of the potatoes crisp too, put the potatoes in the pan and put the lid on. Place a few coals on the lid so the potatoes are cooking from the top and the bottom.

HOT TIPS:

Any potatoes will work here. Try to go for ones on the smaller side so they cook faster.

Always start the potatoes in cold water so they smash and keep together rather than crumbling apart.

Substitute oil for the butter if you are going on a longer camping trip.

Add 2 tbsp of red wine vinegar, 1 bay leaf and ¼ tsp of black peppercorns to the water when boiling the potatoes for an even more delicious flavor.

FIDDLEHEADS (V)

Serves 4

Fiddleheads are the unopened leaves of the ostrich fern. Not all young fern fronds are edible, so make sure you have the right fern. Young fiddlehead fronds are a favorite among foragers. They appear in late spring when the new, emerald green leaves push their tightly furled heads from the papery brown scales of the root stock. The season for fiddleheads is a brief one in late April or early May as the leaves push up through the soil. Once the leaves open, the chance has passed. To enjoy this incredibly delicious woodland delicacy, search for fronds when they are still tightly furled and about 4-6 inches high (10-15 cm). With a sharp knife, just nip the fronds off about half an inch from the curled brown root stock.

Ingredients

- 1 ¼ tsp salt
- 1 clove garlic crushed
- ¼ tsp pepper
- 2 tbsp oil for frying
- 2 cups fiddleheads

Method

Place a pot of water with 1 tsp of the salt on a medium fire. When the water reaches boiling point, add the fiddleheads and boil for 7-10 minutes. Drain the fiddleheads. In a pan, heat the oil and gently wfry the garlic for 30 seconds. Add the fiddleheads and season with the remaining salt and pepper. Fry gently until the edges start to brown —about 3 minutes.

HOT TIPS:

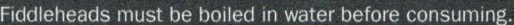

Fiddleheads must be boiled in water before consuming.

You can add them to stews or salads once cooked.

You can keep uncooked fiddleheads in the fridge for up to one week.

Only forage 10% of the available plants so as not to damage the ferns.

BACON-WRAPPED ONION RINGS

Serves 4

This is the best side dish in the history of side dishes. You can make these at home or on the fire and you'll be so glad you did!

Ingredients

- 4 sweet onions
- 1 pack bacon
- ¼ cup Sriracha hot sauce
- ¼ cup mayo
- wooden skewers soaked in water

HOT TIPS:

Use barbecue sauce if you don't like hot sauce.

Method

1. Cut the sweet onions into large rings. You can save the center pieces for use in another recipe. Coat the rings with Sriracha hot sauce and then wrap each ring in bacon (I use two layers.) Poke a skewer through each ring (be sure to secure the ends of the bacon with this so it doesn't come loose during cooking) and place it on a medium fire.

2. Barbecue on both sides until deliciously brown—about 20-25 minutes.

3. Mix the remaining Sriracha hot sauce and the mayo in a bowl for a delicious dipping sauce.

On The Side

BANNOCK

Serves 6

Bannock has been a staple among the Aboriginal people of North America for centuries where it was made from moss, lichen, ground plant bulbs, nut meal, corn meal and cattail pollen to name a few. Consequently, there are as many bannock recipes as the day is long.

The modern version of bannock bread, made from flour, is thought to have been introduced by Scottish fur traders and is featured as a highly prized food item in the journals of the Hudson Bay Company and Northwest Company traders.

Ingredients

- 2 ½ cups flour
- 2 tsp baking powder
- ½ tsp sugar
- ½ tsp salt
- 3 tbsp oil
- 1 cup water

Method

1. Mix dry ingredients. Add oil and enough water to form a firm dough that doesn't stick to the hands. Knead for 3 minutes. Leave to rest for 30 minutes. Scrape some of the coals out from the fire on to the edge of your fire pit so you can cook your bannock.

2. There are a number of ways to cook bannock. You can use a sharp knife to clean the bark off a stick. Break the dough into golf ball-sized chunks. Roll it into a long snake and wrap it around the stick. Hold the stick over the coals, turning frequently until your bannock is brown and cooked through (about 10 minutes).

3. Make fry bread by flattening your golf ball dough balls into disks and frying in oil. Fry bread can be used as a savory vehicle for any filling or sprinkle with cinnamon sugar as a treat that tastes a lot like doughnuts.

4. Make flat bread by dividing the dough into six portions and flattening with the palm of your hand to form discs. Pop the discs directly onto the coals and leave for 3 minutes, then flip over using a pair of tongs. Use the tongs to remove any coals that have stuck to the bread.

CAMPFIRE SKILLET CORNBREAD

Serves 6

The perfect accompaniment to stews, chili and barbecue vegetables.

Ingredients

- 1 cup cornmeal
- ½ cup flour
- 1 tbsp baking powder
- ½ tsp salt
- 1 cup milk (use a powdered milk ratio of 3 tbsp powder to 1 cup water)
- 1 egg
- 2 tbsp honey
- ½ tbsp oil

Method

1. Combine the dry ingredients in a large bowl. Add the milk, egg and honey and mix well with a fork.

2. Over a medium fire, place your camping skillet and add oil. Add the batter and cover with foil or a lid. Cook for 15 minutes or until the edges start to brown.

3. Remove from the heat and leave to cool for 5 minutes with the foil or lid still on.

4. Cut into slices and enjoy!

HOT TIPS:

Substitute 1 tbsp sugar for the honey if it is too difficult to transport to the camp.

On The Side

SOUTH AFRICAN CORNBREAD

Serves 6

This is a recipe I grew up with. In South Africa, this is called mielie bread and the cream corn makes it far moister than traditional corn bread. As such, this doesn't need to be served with chili or stew and can stand alone as a delicious, doughy side. Once you try cornbread this way, you'll never bake it any other way!

Ingredients

- 1 can creamed sweet corn
- 2 eggs (beaten)
- 1 tsp salt
- 2 tbsp (plus 2 tbsp) butter
- ¼ cup warm milk
- 2 ½ cups flour
- 1 tsp baking powder

Method

Place sweet corn, eggs, salt, milk and 2 tbsp butter into a bowl and mix. Mix in flour and baking powder to form a sticky dough. Use the other 2 tbsp butter to grease a Dutch oven. Pour in the dough. Place on a medium fire, put the lid on. Place a couple of coals on the lid for a more even bake. Bake for 45 minutes or until golden brown.

HOT TIPS:

Substitute vegetable shortening for the butter when you are camping and have no cooler.

You can use a skillet or camping pot for this recipe. If you don't have a lid, tent some foil over to keep the heat in.

On The Side

BAKING SODA BREAD

Serves 4

Baking bread is easy and extremely rewarding. If you've never tried it before, you will be happy to see just how simple this is. In the days of yore, everyone baked bread… on a fire! The ability to make fresh bread on any day of a camping trip is a really wonderful superpower to have and will make you a very happy camper.

Ingredients

- 3 cups bread flour
- 3 tsp baking powder
- 1 ¼ tsp salt
- 1 cup water
- 1 tbsp vegetable oil

HOT TIPS:

Brush with egg for a shiny brown finish.

Method

1. In a bowl or camping pot, combine dry ingredients and mix. Stir in water and oil until a sticky dough forms. It is important to work the dough as little as possible.

2. Shape dough and place in a greased camping pot or Dutch oven. Cut an X on the top and sprinkle with a little flour. Place the lid on the pot and pop a few coals on top of the lid so the bread bakes evenly. Bake over a medium fire for 20 minutes or until the edges are brown.

BRAIDED CAMPFIRE BREAD

Serves 6

This bread recipe can be used to make 2 regular loaves, 12 buns or a braided loaf.

Ingredients

- 1 sachet yeast (2 ¼ tsp)
- 3 tbsp sugar
- 2 ¼ cups warm water (100-110°F or 38-43°C)
- 1 tbsp salt
- 2 tbsp oil
- 6.5 cups of flour

HOT TIPS:

Brush with egg for a shiny brown finish.

Method

Mix warm water, yeast and sugar and leave to foam. Once yeast is activated (about 5 minutes) add other ingredients and knead for 8-10 minutes. Place dough in a pot or bowl and cover. Leave in a warm place for 30 minutes or until doubled in size. Knock the dough down and divide into three equal pieces. Roll each piece out into a long snake. Make sure the pieces are the same length. Squeeze all three pieces together at the top, then start to braid. When you get to the bottom, squeeze the bottom pieces together. Place in a lightly oiled Dutch oven or camping pot. Place the lid on the pot and put some coals on the lid for an even bake. Cook over medium coals for 30 minutes or until lightly browned.

SMOKY CAMPFIRE BEANS

Serves 6

Delicious smoky campfire beans that warm you from the inside out. Really great for camping or barbecues.

Ingredients

- 1 can beans
- 3-4 slices bacon
- ½ onion (sliced)
- 1 clove garlic (diced) - optional
- 1 cup ketchup
- 1 cup barbecue sauce
- 2 tbsp brown sugar
- salt and pepper

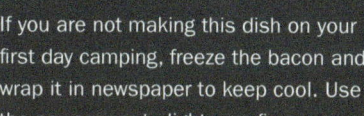

HOT TIPS:

If you are not making this dish on your first day camping, freeze the bacon and wrap it in newspaper to keep cool. Use the newspaper to light your fire.

Method

Cut the bacon into squares and add to the bottom of a camping pot or frying pan. Heat gently over a medium fire to release the fat. Cook, stirring often, for 3 minutes. Add sliced onions and garlic and fry until the bacon and the onions begin to brown (5-7 minutes). Add the ketchup, barbecue sauce, sugar, salt and pepper and heat over a medium fire for 10 minutes, stirring occasionally.

On The Side

BURNT TOMATOES

Serves 4

Slightly burned tomatoes have a great flavor and a little crust that adds to the smokiness of your meal. They make a great side or as an addition to omelets. Of course, there is a huge difference between slightly charred and burned and you want to fall on the right side of that line. Be sure to char them just enough to add color and flavor, but not so much as to ruin the dish.

Ingredients

- 1 punnet cherry tomatoes (250g)
- ½ tsp cracked black pepper
- ½ tsp sugar
- ½ tsp salt
- oil

Method

Place a little oil in the bottom of a camping pan and heat over a medium fire until warm. Slice the tomatoes in half and sprinkle with sugar and salt. Place them cut side down on your pan and leave them to fry until a black rim forms around the edges – about 3 minutes. Season with cracked black pepper and serve hot.

HOT TIPS:

Don't move the tomatoes around or they will burst and burn. You can use full-sized tomatoes if you prefer. Cooking times will be longer.

On The Side

More Hot Tips

PACKING, COOLING AND STORING FOOD

Freeze your food before you leave, especially meat and cheese products. Keep things frozen longer by packing them in foil cold bags or wrapping them in newspaper. Use the newspaper to start your fires when you get to your campsite. You can further insulate your frozen foods by wrapping them in clothing and stashing in the middle of your backpack.

SQUARE

Planning to stay on one campsite? Take small coolers if you can. Pack one for each two-day food cycle so that you aren't opening the cooler all the time. If you're on the move, pack a flattened cardboard box. At your campsite, reconstruct the box, then place your newspaper-wrapped frozen items in it. You can further insulate with clothing. Place in a shady spot.

CLOVE HITCH

Always (always!) hang your food. Losing a couple of meals (and possibly other bits) to wild animals will ruin your trip in two shakes of a raccoon's tail. Never keep food in your tent. Hang food by throwing a rope over a branch that is at least 200 feet (60 meters) from your campsite. Tie the rope to your pack and hoist it at least 12-15 feet (3.5 to 4.5 meters) into the air. Tie off the rope with one of these handy knots:

BOW LINE

Use sand to remove stubborn food from the bottom of pots and bury the sand (with your suds) far away from your campsite.

HOW TO FILLET A FISH

Yay you caught a fish! Well done Indiana Jones, now you can really impress your camp buddies by cleaning it and serving it for dinner. It's easy, just take your time and work carefully and you will master this great life skill in no time.

Remove the scales first. Hold the fish by the tail and, with the back of your knife, scrape from the tail to the head. The scales should fly off. Lay the fish flat on the cutting board with its spine facing you. Locate the dorsal fin just above the gills. Hold the knife at a 45 angle, next to the dorsal fin, with the bottom tilted to the fish head. Make a single cut down across the width of the fish from spine to belly. Cut down to the spine, but not thorough it. Now angle the knife the other way and slice down the length of the fish from gill to tail so you have one solid fillet. Repeat on the other side for your second fillet. Rinse the fillets in cold water.

HOW TO CLEAN A FISH

If you want to cook the whole fish, it's easier to clean. Remove the scales first. Hold the fish by the tail and, with the back of your knife, scrape from the tail to the head. The scales should fly off. Cut off the dorsal fins using two 45° angle cuts on both sides of the fin. Lay the fish on its side with the belly facing you.

Lay one hand on the top of the fish and then cut through the middle of the belly from the gills to the tail. Reach in and remove the innards. Wash the whole fish and cavity with cold water. Your fish is ready to cook!

Note: Be responsible when discarding scales and innards. Dig a hole to bury them and ensure that you don't create a mess in the campsite for the next campers to deal with. Wildlife may also be attracted to the smell of fresh fish, so discard bits you don't want away from your campsite.

GREEN MOXIE

ADVENTURES IN SUSTAINABLE LIVING

It's tough to get people to care about something they don't have a personal connection too. That's why Greenmoxie was created—to get people and their kids off the couch and into the woods. Greenmoxie is an environmental blog that provides eco-living tips so you can live a life that's leaner, greener and more sustainable. We help you grow your own food, forage, preserve, recycle and upcycle and make all your own cleaning products and cosmetics so you save Mother Nature and a little cash too.

FROM THE GREENMOXIE SHOP

We have created and curated an incredible collection of things we use or make ourselves. Here are some of our excellent products for you and your family. You can find all these wonderful wares on our website:

store.greenmoxie.com

OH SH!T KIT

With the Oh Sh!t kit, you'll be prepared for everything Mother Nature throws at you. From bug bites, to sunburn, we've got you covered. This personal first aid kit is made from all natural and organic herbs. Comes in a cotton carrying bag.

SPICE POUCH

Made from leather, the Greenmoxie Camping Spice Pouch holds three spice bottles with corks. Choose from pink Himalayan salt, steak rub, rib rub, taco spice, Striratcha spice, pepper, basil and salt.

Now Go Outside...

...OR KEEP ON READING WITH THESE OTHER BOOKS BY THE SAME AUTHOR

www.ingramcontent.com/pod-product-compliance
Lightning Source LLC
Chambersburg PA
CBHW051600010526
44118CB00023B/2768